D0622382

TEAM SPIRIT!™

CHEERLEADING

Lynn Singer

rosen
central™

The Rosen Publishing Group, Inc., New York

Published in 2007 by The Rosen Publishing Group, Inc.
29 East 21st Street, New York, NY 10010

Library of Congress Cataloging-in-Publication Data

Singer, Lynn.
Cheerleading/Lynn Singer.
    p. cm.—(Team spirit!)
Includes bibliographical references and index.
ISBN 1-4042-0728-7 (library binding)
1. Cheerleading.
I. Title. II. Series: Team spirit! (New York, N.Y.) III. Series.
LB3635.S56 2006
791.6'4–dc22

2005037504

Manufactured in the United States of America

On the cover: Members of the Fairport High School cheerleading squad
from Fairport, New York, perform a basket toss stunt on the sidelines during
a football game in September 2005.

CONTENTS

THE SPIRIT OF CHEERLEADING

It's a crisp Friday night in October. The stadium lights shine bright as the stands fill to capacity with excited fans anticipating the start of the big game. As the marching band plays spirited music, the sea of spectators dressed in black and green is on its feet waving spirit towels and shaking pom pons. It is homecoming—the most important game of the season, played against the school's fiercest rival. Alumni have returned to cheer their alma mater. Parents and grandparents are proudly positioned as they await the performance of their children and grandchildren. Little brothers wear the jerseys of their football-playing big brothers. And little sisters dress up as cheerleaders in look-alike skirts and sweaters.

College cheerleaders, such as the team at the University of Texas, rev up crowds from the sidelines by performing exciting stunts and leading chants and cheers.

The cheerleaders take their place at the goal line holding a huge victory banner that invites the football team to crash through and enter the stadium. The crowd sends up a deafening yell, the band blasts the school fight song, and the football players charge on to the field through the lineup of their biggest fans: the cheerleaders.

With the kickoff, the game is on. On the sidelines, the cheerleaders orchestrate the crowd in battle cries of "Go, Fight, Win" and "Touchdown, Touchdown, Six Points Now!" They're ready for four quarters of nonstop spirit. Whether the home team plays a great game or a bad game, whether they win or lose, the cheerleaders are there to motivate the crowd to join in chants; entertain the crowd with feats of tumbling, stunts, and dances; and coordinate the efforts of the band, dance team, mascot, and flag corps all for the benefit of school spirit and pride.

Cheerleading has evolved into more than just leading cheers at sporting events. Where it once was considered a popularity contest, cheerleading now requires serious training, skill development, and dedication. Today, it is an athletic activity in and of itself. Some even say cheerleading is a sport. Like the athletes they support, cheerleaders must be strong, in shape, and well trained in the skills and techniques they perform. They have to be able to tumble, stunt, jump, dance, and perform cheers and chants with accuracy.

Over the years, the role of cheerleaders has expanded. Begun as a way to raise school spirit and increase student participation and spectatorship at games, cheerleading eventually entered the realm of

Cheerleaders spend hours training and perfecting skills to cheer their teams. The athletic ability of cheerleaders continues to evolve, and cheerleading is now considered a sport of its own with competitions and titles.

competitive sports. Today, cheerleading squads compete for national titles and trophies, just like the football and basketball teams they support. Competitive cheerleading has raised the bar for the skill level and abilities required to join the ranks of these athletes.

It begins in gymnastics gyms, dance studios, weight-training facilities, and aerobics classes. It can start as early as age five. The preparation and conditioning is strenuous and focused. Cheerleading is no longer just a youthful activity; it can become a career. Are you ready for the challenge? Read on for all the steps it takes to become a cheerleader and the lifelong lessons and benefits cheerleading can provide. Great people who have done great things in our world were once cheerleaders. Maybe cheerleading will prepare you for greatness, too!

CHAPTER 1

THE EVOLUTION OF CHEERLEADING

Cheerleading is the coordinated effort of encouraging and organizing the spirit and participation of spectators in support of a sports team. It is also a competitive event in which squads vie against each other for rankings and awards. Nearly every high school in the United States has a cheerleading team. All across the country, little girls dream of someday being one of those

Cheerleading is as American as apple pie. Many little girls set their sights on inspiring school spirit by becoming a cheerleader.

jumping, flipping, and spirited athletes.

A Brief History of Cheerleading

It all started at a Princeton-Rutgers football game in 1869, when residents of Princeton University's Nassau Hall yelled "Sis Boom Rah!" in locomotive style. And the first recorded yell by the later-formed pep club at Princeton was "Ray, Ray, Ray! Tiger, Tiger, Tiger! Sis, Sis, Sis! Boom, Boom, Boom! Aaaaah, Princeton! Princeton! Princeton!"

Thomas Peebles, a graduate of Princeton, took the "Ray, Ray, Ray!" yell to the University of Minnesota in 1884. By 1898, a University of

Minnesota medical student named Johnny Campbell organized the election of six "yell leaders" for the last football game of the season, and the first organized cheerleading squad was formed. Its yell was "Rah, Rah, Rah! Ski-U-Mah! Hoo-Rah! Hoo-Rah! Varsity! Varsity! Minn-e-so-tah!" Johnny Campbell's yell leaders incorporated coordinated yells and the school fight song, introduced the megaphone, and boosted school spirit and game attendance.

The first yell leaders were men, and for years, cheerleading was an all-male activity. The yell leaders, who were also known as rooter kings, wore wool sweaters, pants, and "bucks," which are like saddle shoes. Women became involved in cheerleading during World War II, when many young men were away serving in the armed services. Since then, females have dominated the sport, although there are still many males who participate. Today, roughly 90 percent of cheerleaders are women.

The very first summer cheerleading camp was held at Sam Houston State Teacher's College (now Sam Houston State University) in 1948. Lawrence R. Herkimer, a former cheerleader at Southern Methodist University, organized the camp of fifty-two students. Three years later, Herkimer formed the National Cheerleaders Association, teaching cheerleading skills at summer camps across the nation. He also created the "Herkie" jump (one leg bent, one leg extended, one arm in the air, and the other on the hip) and invented the pom pon (commonly, though incorrectly, referred to as the pom pom). Herkimer is fondly referred to as the grandfather of cheerleading and is largely responsible for fostering the popularity and progression of cheerleading.

Male cheerleaders started it all. Men like these yell leaders from Yale University, shown here in 1930, were the first cheerleaders and dominated the activity until women joined squads in the 1940s.

Summer camp instructional programs gained in popularity in the 1950s and 1960s, spreading the cheerleading phenomenon from coast to coast. The 1970s brought the evolution of partner stunts and pyramids, and the incorporation of dance and elite tumbling, all broadening the range of skills and difficulty displayed in cheerleading. The 1970s also saw the passage of Title IX, a law that ordered gender equality in middle schools and high schools. Title IX is widely recognized as being instrumental in the development of women's sports. As cheerleading

Herkie's History

Name: Lawrence R. Herkimer

Born: October 14, 1925, in Dallas, Texas

High School: North Dallas High School; cheered all four years

College: Southern Methodist University; cheered his first year, did a two-year tour in the navy during World War II, then returned to cheer for two more years.

Cheer Credits

- Created the Herkie jump.
- Conducted the first ever summer cheerleading clinic in 1948.
- Formally incorporated the National Cheerleaders Association (NCA) in 1951.
- Invented the pom pon after seeing color television for the first time at the New York World's Fair in 1956.
- Created the Spirit Stick as the coveted summer camp award for teamwork and enthusiasm in 1957.

Fun Facts from the 1950s and 1960s

- Appeared in Sports Illustrated doing the Herkie jump and became known as Mr. Cheerleader. Appeared on game shows including *To Tell the Truth*, *Truth or Consequences*, and *What's My Line?*
- Appeared in a Cheer detergent commercial.

Lawrence Herkimer performs his signature Herkie jump over the heads of his summer camp instructors. Cheerleaders all over the world today learn the Herkie as one of the fundamental jumps in cheer skill building.

was becoming more and more athletic and women's sports began to gain an equal footing with traditional men's sports, the cheerleader's job expanded to include cheering at women's sports.

The very first National Collegiate Cheerleading Championships were televised on CBS in 1978, and competitive cheerleading was born. Local, regional, and national championships were organized by a number of cheerleading companies, and in 1983, ESPN began airing UCA's (Universal Cheerleaders Association) National High School Cheerleading Championships. Competitive cheerleading pushed skill levels to new heights in the 1980s and 1990s, leading to the creation of all-star cheerleading gyms and the new concept of training cheerleaders for the sole purpose of competing. In 2004, the U.S. All-Star Federation (an organization of cheerleading competition companies serving as the governing body of All-Star cheerleading), hosted the Cheerleading Worlds, billed as "the last stop" in the competition season. Winning teams from several national championships came together to compete for the first ever world title in cheerleading.

From the spontaneous "Sis Boom Rah!" yell at the Princeton-Rutgers football game to the early yell leaders at the University of Minnesota and the fully organized summer camps started by Lawrence Herkimer, cheerleading has evolved into an athletic activity requiring versatile individual skill, sophisticated coaching, dedication, and teamwork.

CHAPTER 2

Skills and Making the Team

While the common purpose of school cheerleading squads is to raise school spirit and serve as ambassadors for their school, cheerleading styles are different in various regions of the country. Most squads lead simple, repetitive chants on the sidelines of sports games that the crowd can join in and respond to. They also perform cheers during time-outs

Jumps are an integral part of cheerleading and add excitement to cheers and performances. This cheerleading instructor executes a jump called the front hurdler.

and halftimes that allow the squad to show its skill in stunting and tumbling. Some states or school districts restrict the performance of stunting in cheerleading. Cheer squads also dance to school fight songs and use pom pons, megaphones, and signs to encourage crowd involvement. With the increase in competitive cheerleading, squads incorporate all of those elements (cheer, dance, stunting, and tumbling) into one routine at state and national competitions.

Cheer teams can range from as few as five to more than thirty members. The size is usually dictated by the purpose of the team. Teams that cheer at wrestling matches and volleyball games, for example, most likely won't be stunting and tumbling because of space constraints. Their focus will be cheering for the athletes and leading the crowd through responsive chants. These teams will have fewer members, or a larger team may divide into smaller units and rotate at various sporting events. Teams that compete need members who can fill all specialties, from stunting to dancing to tumbling. These teams average between fifteen and twenty-five members, but they can range from six to thirty-five members.

A cheerleader is a versatile athlete and must be skilled in several areas in order to make the squad. These areas include motions, jumps, dance, stunting, tumbling, and voice. Here is a list of some of the most basic techniques.

Motions

A motion is a hand or arm position that is used in a cheer. Motions make a cheer visible to and effective for a crowd by accentuating the words and rhythm. Motions must be executed with proper placement and a lot of strength. The following are some basic motions that all cheerleaders must know.

Hand Positions

- **Fist** A cheerleading fist is made by closing your fingers to the palm of your hand and wrapping your thumb on top of your fingers, with the wrists held straight and tight.
- **Blade** A blade is made by extending the fingers straight, while kept together, with the thumb tucked in.

Motions add visual effect to cheers and dances and are one of the first skill sets a cheerleader learns. Proper execution is always strong and crisp. This Step One cheerleader demonstrates the high V.

Arm Motions

- **High V** Arms are extended up forming a *V*, with the hands in fists or blades, the wrists held straight, and the knuckles or palms facing down.

- **Low V** Arms are extended down forming an inverted *V*. Hands are in fists or blades, with the wrists held straight and the palms facing down.

- **Touchdown** Arms are extended straight up and parallel to each other.

- **T motion** Both arms are extended straight out to the side and parallel to the ground.

- **Diagonal** One arm is extended as in a high V, while the other arm is extended as in a low V.

Jumps

Jumps add to the excitement of cheerleading, especially when celebrating a touchdown and motivating a crowd. A properly executed jump will have good height and correct midair position, show flexibility, and finish with a solid landing. Here is a partial list of cheerleading jumps, in order of increasing difficulty.

- **Tuck jump** A jump during which the cheerleader pulls the knees up toward the chest at a 90-degree angle, while forming a high V, keeping the head and back straight.
- **Spread eagle** While jumping, the body makes an *X* in the air. Knees and shoelaces face forward.
- **Herkie** A jump with one leg extended straight to the side with knee facing upward and the other leg bent with the knee pointing down and the bottom of the foot facing up.
- **Toe touch** In midair, legs are extended straight to each side, with the toes pointed, the knees facing upward, and the arms in a *T* motion.
- **Pike** In midair, both legs are extended forward, with knees facing upward and toes pointed. The body bends to meet the legs, with the arms held parallel to the legs and head up.

Dance

Dance is an element that has evolved as an important cheerleading skill. Cheerleaders dance to school fight songs, perform energetic dances during time-outs and halftimes to entertain the crowd, and incorporate dance sections in competition routines to show the versatility of a squad. "Cheer-dance" is a unique style that incorporates cheerleading arm motions. It is usually very fast-paced and often includes hip-hop or other urban dance techniques. Pom pons are sometimes used to add color and visual effect to the choreography. In preparing for tryouts and to improve skills, cheerleaders may take hip-hop classes at dance studios to learn rhythm, placement, and how to dance as part of a group.

Stunting

Stunting refers to the combined skill of three or more cheerleaders performing a mount or climb to build a group or pyramid. It is a thrilling part of cheerleading and a crowd favorite. To ensure the safety of the team members, it is important for all the performers to learn the basics first, progress to more advance stunts and pyramids, and train with a coach who is certified by a cheerleading safety organization, such as the American Association of Cheerleading Coaches and Advisors (AACCA), the National Council for Spirit Safety and Education (NCSSE), and the U.S. All-Star Federation (USASF). The National

Stunting is the skill that every cheerleader can't wait to perform. Following safety guidelines and skill progression under the supervision of a trained and certified coach is imperative for stunt success.

Federation of State High School Associations (NFHS) publishes safety guidelines for sports, including the publication *Spirit*, which includes rules for cheerleading and dance teams. Many states follow these guidelines.

Stunts can be held at shoulder level or extended above the head. More advanced stunts highlight the top person, or "flyer," standing on one leg while holding the other leg in a variety of positions, either hooked at the knee, lifted out to the side in a "heel stretch," held behind the body while facing the side in an "arabesque," or held with the hands behind the head in a "scorpion."

Safe and successful stunting requires complete trust and cooperation among the participants. Each cheerleader has a specific responsibility to assure the stability of the stunt. Even though most teams are made up of girls, stunts and pyramids can be enhanced by a boy's strength. The lifting, tossing, and overall display of strength in stunting can excel with the addition of boys. Based on individual strengths and abilities, each squad member will be assigned to one of these stunt positions:

- **Top person** Also called the flyer, this is the person on top of a stunt, pyramid, or toss.
- **Base** The person(s) that holds, lifts, or tosses a top person into a stunt. The base is usually standing and provides primary support for another person. When a stunt involves more than one base, the main base has the most control over the top person and in some stunts is directly below the top person. The secondary base

is positioned across from the main base and will usually help support the foot (single leg stunt) or hold one of the feet (double leg stunt) of the top person.

- **Spotter** A person whose primary responsibility is the protection of another during the performance of a skill. A spotter watches the stability of the top person and is always prepared to assist the bases should more strength be required to hold a stunt or to catch the top person should a fall occur.

- **Back spot** This is the cheerleader in the back of the stunt who is mainly responsible for protecting the head and shoulders of the top person during a controlled dismount or fall.

- **Front spot** This is the person who is in position to add strength to keep a stunt stable or to add height to a toss. The front spot is not involved in the cradling process (catching the flyer as she dismounts from the top of a stunt or comes down from a toss).

Gymnastics/Tumbling

Tumbling is a specialty in cheerleading that includes acrobatic and gymnastics skills, such as back handsprings and flips. Not all squad members will have the same amount of gymnastics training, so the skill levels within a squad will vary. Some squads have a tradition of performing a series of back handsprings in the end zone to celebrate a touchdown. Others incorporate tumbling when they enter and exit the basketball court for a time-out or halftime performance. Tumbling is an

important part of competition routines. Here is a partial list of tumbling skills that most cheerleaders will learn:

- **Forward roll** A forward roll begins in a squat position with the knees held together and both hands flat on the floor in front of the body. The roll is executed by tucking the head down while pushing with the legs, supporting the weight with the arms, and rolling on the shoulders to return to the beginning position.

- **Backward roll** The backward roll also begins in a squat position. The roll is executed by dropping the heels, rolling through the shoulders, placing the hands flat on the floor with fingers toward the shoulders, and then pushing off the floor to complete the skill and return to the beginning position.

- **Cartwheel** A cartwheel can be executed either to the left or to the right. For a left cartwheel, from a standing position, reach down with the left hand, placing it on the floor in line with the left foot, then kick the right leg as the right hand is placed on the floor in line with the left hand. Follow with the left leg then land on the right leg.

- **Round-off** The round-off begins with a push-off on one leg, followed by swinging the legs upward in a fast cartwheel motion

Safety guidelines for college cheerleaders allow more difficult stunts and tosses than are allowed at the high school level. Georgetown University cheerleaders *(left)* entertain the crowd at an NCAA basketball game with a basket toss with back tuck.

into a 90-degree turn. It finishes with both feet landing at the same time.

- **Back walkover** The back walkover begins in a standing position with arms over the head and one leg extended forward. The walkover is executed by bending backward, placing the hands on the floor while pushing off the supporting leg, and kicking the working leg over. The skill ends by landing on the working leg, following with the supporting leg, and returning to a standing position.

- **Back handspring** Also known as the flip-flop or the flic-flac, the back handspring begins in a standing position with arms overhead. The arms swing down as the knees bend, and the move is continued by springing off the floor back onto the hands, pushing quickly from the hands, and swinging the legs over to return to the feet.

- **Standing back tuck** The skill begins in a standing position and is executed with an uplift, tuck, and inverted rotation of the body, landing in a standing position. Hands do not touch the floor during execution.

As Chris Korotky, publisher of *Inside Gymnastics* and *Inside Cheerleading* magazines, advises in an interview with the author of this book, "Always train with a qualified coach who can teach you proper execution and technique. Safety is important, especially when learning a new skill." Once basic tumbling is learned, the skills can be linked together in succession: for example, round-off, back handspring or round-off, back handspring, back tuck.

Gymnastics and tumbling skills are incorporated into all aspects of cheerleading, whether along the sidelines of a game or in a competition performance. Cheerleaders train at gymnastics and all-star cheerleading gyms to master tumbling techniques. The progression of difficulty leads to the back tuck, performed by a University of Texas cheerleader (above) at a football game.

Voice

Obviously, vocalizing is a fundamental aspect of cheerleading. After all, cheerleading started with a yell. Chants and cheers must be yelled with a crisp, loud, deep voice so that the crowd can both hear and understand the words that are being said. A clear voice expresses confidence and excitement. There is a technique for using

Girls and boys hoping to make the cheerleading team can't wait to be in uniform in front of a crowd. Calling out the chants and cheers to hear the crowd respond is all part of the fun.

your voice. When practicing vocals, the power and energy should come from the diaphragm, which is located at the bottom of the ribcage. Put your hand on your diaphragm while practicing a chant or cheer. You should feel the muscles contract, or push in, sharply with each word. This exercise will make your voice louder and deeper and will protect your vocal cords from strain. A cheerleader must be careful not to lose his or her voice.

Squad Tryouts

Cheerleading is harder than it looks. Becoming a good cheerleader takes a lot of practice. To have the best chance of making the squad, some training is very helpful. You don't have to have all the skills before tryouts, but an introduction to the basics will put you a step ahead. There are several places to learn cheerleading skills before you try out for a school squad. Look for cheerleading gyms, gymnastics gyms, or dance studios in your neighborhood that offer cheerleading classes.

Also, many high school squads offer cheerleading clinics throughout the year for junior high schools and elementary schools as a pretraining for girls and boys hoping to become high school cheerleaders. Some high schools even offer cheerleading classes for physical education credit to train students who want to try out for the squad.

There is usually some paperwork that must be processed before you can join a cheerleading squad. This typically includes an application, a medical release, and a parental permission form. Your application shows your interest in and commitment to becoming a cheerleader. Most squads set a minimum grade point average required to qualify for tryouts, and some squads require teacher recommendations that confirm your good conduct in class. The medical release is signed by your doctor and confirms that you are in good health. The parent permission form shows the coach that your parents support your desire to become a squad member.

Most schools hold mandatory clinics or practices to teach the skills required for making the squad. Clinics are typically held after school for several days, culminating in the actual tryout. The material taught varies from school to school, but it usually includes a cheer to show your motion and voice technique, jumps, a dance, and sometimes tumbling. Everyone will learn the same material at the clinics.

Tryout Day

On the day of the tryout, you will show off your skills in front of a panel of judges who are local cheerleading experts. These experts may include the squad coach, coaches of other school teams, cheerleaders at a nearby college or university, or instructors from a cheerleading organization or gym.

Everyone will be required to wear the same style of clothing—usually shorts, T-shirt or sports bra, and supportive athletic shoes. You'll be assigned a number and will try out in groups of three to five candidates, usually in the school gymnasium. Most tryouts are "closed," allowing no one in the gym during the session except for the group and the judges.

There may be callbacks after everyone has tried out. This means that the judges want to take another look at some of the athletes trying out for the squad. A callback usually occurs when judges are trying to decide between a few athletes for a particular spot on the squad. If the athletes weren't part of the same tryout group, it is often helpful for the judges to see them side by side to compare skill level.

There are many ways coaches announce who has made the new team. Your coach may make the announcement to the entire group as soon as tryouts are over. Or, you may be sent home after tryouts and the coach will call the new members of the team to congratulate them. Other coaches post a list at the school at a specified time after tryouts are over. Whatever method your coach uses, it's an exciting day for some and disappointing for others. Prepare yourself for either outcome. If you make the team, great! If you don't, try again next year, or participate in another activity that matches your interests and skills.

Making a Commitment and Working as a Team

Making the squad means making a huge commitment. As a cheerleader, you will be part of a group that is counting on you to be successful. You're committing to be at every practice, game, and performance. You're committing to always learning, improving, and perfecting your skills. You're committing to putting yourself second, and your teammates first. Good grades, excellent school citizenship, following the rules, and representing your school in the most positive ways are all part of committing to your squad.

It is often said that a chain is only as strong as its weakest link. A cheerleading squad will stay strong only if each squad member lives up to his or her commitments.

CHAPTER
3

Practice

Practice makes perfect, and perfection in cheerleading is achieved when a squad performs as a unit, which means every member must perform with equal and uniform technique. The only way to achieve that level is to practice hard. Your coach will lead you through skill drills in squad practice, encourage team spirit through team-building activities, and take you through focused training at a summer camp.

It takes lots of practice and training to become a cheerleader. Making the squad takes discipline, dedication and a commitment to skill development.

Squad Practice

Practicing as a squad will hone your technique. During squad practice, you will learn the chants, cheers, and routines that you will perform at games and in competitions. Skill drills are an important part of squad practice. They are used to help you memorize the name and execution of each technique and skill so that the movement becomes second nature by the time you perform. Just as football players learn a playbook and basketball players practice free throws, cheerleaders learn and repeat fundamentals and techniques before progressing on to advanced skills and full routines.

Cheer squads often perform with pom pons, megaphones, and spirit signs. Once a cheer or dance is learned, you'll practice how to handle the equipment that is a part of that choreography. The goal is to feel like the prop is a part of your body. You should be able to control pom pons and signs as easily as you control your arms and hands. Using these props in practice is necessary to their being used effectively in front of a crowd.

Part of handling props effectively includes what to do with them before and after you use them in a routine or cheer. Props should be placed safely and neatly away from the main performance area until you're ready to use them. If you set aside the props during a performance, be sure that they are returned safely and neatly away from the performance area. An out-of-place megaphone or other prop is distracting to the crowd and presents a danger to the squad while performing.

Team Spirit

Not only do cheerleaders have to perform as a unified team, they have to think and act as a unified team. A successful cheerleading squad consists of individuals who put the good of the team first, trust each other, and understand the importance of team unity.

There's a common saying among cheerleaders: "There is no *I* in team." It is a perfect reminder that, while made up of individuals, a team only works when everyone sets his or her individuality aside and identifies with the group. You learn how to put the good of the team first by asking yourself questions like, If I don't show up for practice today, will that help or hurt the team? If I don't do my part in learning this new

Summer cheerleading camp is a great time for a team to learn new skills, build teamwork, and get to know each other. Camps are typically held on college campuses and consist of an intense three or four days of training. Teams sometimes bring instructors to their schools for a private camp, customized for their needs.

stunt, will that help or hurt the team? If I gossip about one of my teammates, will that help or hurt the team? Putting the good of the team first may mean doing some things you do not enjoy, but the team will benefit by your doing them.

As a cheer squad trains together, a great deal of trust is built among the members of the squad, especially while learning how to stunt. Each cheerleader has an important responsibility when building a stunt, and every squad member has to trust that every other squad member is doing his or her job so that the stunt is stable and safe. You're putting your safety in the hands of your teammates, and you're asking them to put their safety in your hands. When you have that trust and confidence in each other, nothing is impossible.

The result of putting the team first and learning to trust each other is team unity. Mixing a variety of personalities that are all focused on the same goals and have the same motivation is the best recipe for creating team spirit.

Cheer Camp

Summer camp is the perfect place for cheer squads to drill fundamentals, learn material for the upcoming year, and bond as a team. "It brings you back to the basics," says Darren Thompson, director of project development for Cheer Ltd., a cheer company based in Fayetteville, North Carolina. "As with any sport or activity, the basic building blocks are essential to the highest level of performance in cheerleading." There are many companies across the country that offer a wide variety of summer camp programs. Camps are often held on college campuses and last two to four days. These are usually open to everyone. Some schools hold private camps for their students only.

What to Expect

If your squad chooses to go to a camp on a college campus, you're in for a lot of fun and a lot of hard work. This is a very short period of time

All-star cheerleading gyms such as World Cup All-Stars in Freehold, New Jersey, have full-time coaches who teach tumbling and cheerleading skills to teams and individuals year-round. They also train cheerleaders to become part of competition teams.

to learn cheerleading basics, cheers, chants, stunting, tumbling, dance, and team building. It will also be your first introduction to competition, as performances will be evaluated throughout the camp.

You'll stay in the dorms on campus, eat in the college cafeteria, and participate in a variety of cheerleading classes. Classes are typically divided by technique and/or ability level so that every participant is able to learn at a pace in line with his or her skill level. Classes run the spectrum of conditioning, fundamentals, jumps, stunts, cheers, chants,

Captain Qualities

Being the leader of your peers isn't always easy. It's difficult balancing friendships while you're also trying to fulfill your duties as captain of the team. The pressure is on to lead by example, discipline your teammates when needed, solve problems, motivate, and follow the directions of your coach. It's a tough job, but with hard work, you can be a great captain for your team. Here's a checklist of the top qualities every captain needs:

- Always look for solutions to problems rather than looking to blame someone who caused them.
- Treat all your teammates equally.
- Plan ahead.
- Listen to your coach.
- Accept constructive criticism.
- Be consistent.
- Give credit to those who deserve it.
- Always be willing to improve.

dances, team building, captain's classes, and more. Evaluations are held each day to measure a squad's progression, with final evaluations held on the last day of camp, recognizing squads that improve and excel. Many camp companies also award bids to squads to compete at their national championships.

Why It's Great

Summer camp is like an intense boot camp for cheerleaders. Hard work, sweat, sore muscles, and little sleep are all a part of it. However, in a surprisingly short period of time, you'll learn and improve more than you thought possible.

One of the best features of camp is the opportunity it provides for getting to know your teammates better. You spend all day and night with your squad learning cheerleading and learning about each other. Evening squad pizza parties, activities planned by the camp host, and even introducing yourselves to the squad from your rival school all create memories to last a lifetime!

Another great part of camp is that you find out exactly how much you're capable of. Classes are challenging but fun, and you see quick improvement in your abilities. Learning alongside other teams and being exposed to other styles of cheerleading and new choreography ideas can all benefit your squad by challenging you to try new things. Your squad may have traditions and standards that are important to maintain, but great squads are always looking for new ideas and ways to evolve.

CHAPTER 4

Performance

Cheer squads perform at a variety of games and events. Each has its own purpose, function, requirements, and limitations. The most common school-related performances are pep rallies and various sporting events. However, most cheerleading squads dream of winning various regional and national competitions. Cheerleading competitions have grown in popularity over the last fifteen

Performing is such an exciting part of cheer-leading. Whether it's game day, a pep rally, or a competition, each performance requires a different role from the cheerleading squad.

years, with many national competitions being televised.

Pep Rallies

Cheerleaders have a big responsibility at pep rallies. Whether it's a weekly pep rally for the football team, a special rally for home-coming, or a general pep rally celebrating overall school spirit, cheerleaders are there to lead and engage the student body in chants, entertain by dancing to the school fight song, and impress the crowd with specialty skills such as tumbling and stunting. Cheerleaders often lead skits depicting the home team defeating their rivals and work with the faculty to plan rallies that raise school pride and encourage attendance at upcoming games or activities.

Games

Football and basketball (both boys' and girls') are the two sports where you'll most commonly find cheerleaders. Volleyball players, wrestlers, and track athletes also enjoy encouragement from cheerleaders at games and meets.

The main responsibility of the cheer squad is to involve the crowd in chants for the team. The captain will start the chant, the squad will join in, and the crowd will follow. As long as the chant is short and repetitive, it will be easy for the crowd to learn and participate. The cheerleaders have to pay close attention to the game and be familiar with the rules of each sport to be sure they are leading the appropriate chant for the current action or situation. For example, when the team is playing defense in a football game, the cheerleaders want to be careful not to start a chant for the offense.

To show good sportsmanship, the cheer squad from the home team will go to the visitor's side to welcome the visiting cheer squad. Sometimes squads exchange small gifts or even participate in a dance or cheer together.

Cheer squads will have special cheers or dances prepared for time-outs and halftimes. When the marching band or pep band starts playing the fight song or other spirited music, the cheerleaders will perform a dance. This is an opportunity for the cheerleaders to entertain the crowd and keep them spirited until the sports teams return to the game.

Competitive cheerleading is the fastest-growing segment of cheerleading today. More than 3,500 all-star gyms nationwide train teams to compete in local, state, regional, and national championships. Pro Spirit, Inc., from McKinney, Texas, is shown in competition at the America's Best All-Star Cheer & Dance National Championship.

Competitions

Competitive cheerleading has gained in popularity, especially in the last fifteen years. State spirit associations conduct competitions for school teams and many companies conduct regional and national championships annually. There are many options if your squad chooses to compete. Competitions range from small, local events held in school gymnasiums with several squads to large, national events held at theme parks and convention centers with hundreds of squads from across the country.

Just as your squad learns basic skills before progressing to more advanced skills, it is smart for a squad to begin competing at smaller events before attending a larger, national event.

Whatever the size of the event, there are common factors for every competition. Whether hosted by a state spirit association or a competition company, each organizing group sets its own performance requirements, which dictate the elements to be included in a routine. Safety guidelines will be set and most likely will follow guidelines established by one of the national safety organizations.

Most competitions take place on gymnastics mats. Spring floors, which are gymnastics mats with a series of strong springs beneath them, add to the safety of the competition and are common at larger events.

Squads compete in divisions such as varsity, junior varsity, and junior high. Often, competing squads are grouped by ability level so that novice teams and advanced teams have the opportunity to compete with squads at the same skill level. Each ability level has its own set of restrictions for stunting and tumbling to make sure that squads compete safely. It is important that squads compete up to, but not past, their ability level.

Winning and Losing

On any given day, a squad can have its best performance or its worst performance. Part of the competition process is learning how to win and lose. Winning is great, but it's not what competition is all about. The competition is about the work your team puts into the months of practice preparing for it. It's about the victory you experience when you learn a new skill or perfect a new stunt or make it through a dance with no mistakes. If you go into a competition with the attitude of learning rather than the expectation of winning, you'll experience what it really means to win. Here are a few of the things that set an example for good sportsmanship at a competition:

- Represent your school with only the best and most respectable behavior toward your squad and others.
- Be genuinely excited and appreciative of any award you receive. Whether it's tenth place or first place, accept it with enthusiasm.
- If you're the team that comes in second place, stand up and congratulate the first-place team. Send them a congratulatory note after the competition.
- If your team wins, take time to congratulate the other teams on a great performance. Be gracious winners.
- If an award isn't earned, congratulate the other teams and focus on areas needing improvement. Even if you don't agree with the judges' decision, those are the results for that day. Stay positive and study your score sheets to prepare for next time.

Uniforms

What to wear on game day and at competitions is very important for a cheerleading squad. Uniform design and function sure have come a long way since the early days of cheerleading. In the 1950s, the universal

A first-place trophy isn't the only prize competitive cheerleaders can receive. The training process leading up to a competition provides the benefits of advancing skill development, building team trust, self-discipline, and good sportsmanship.

uniform worn by cheerleaders was a wool sweater decorated with the school initials, an ankle-length skirt, bobby socks, and saddle shoes. Advancing cheerleading skills, clothing fashion trends, and new fabric technology have all influenced what cheerleaders wear today. Squads often have multiple uniforms for different types of performances. A squad might have a uniform to wear for football games or outdoor sports, a second uniform for basketball games or indoor sports, and even a third uniform that is more decorated and flashy for competitions.

Some uniform companies even work with coaches to design a custom uniform that no other squad will have.

"The biggest trends in cheerleading fashion right now are sequin braid and lettering, briefs made of sequin and other specialty fabrics, custom logos and lettering for the front of tops and coordinating a uniform with warm-ups, bags, and hair bows to create an entire 'spirit wardrobe' for a team," explains Kevin Jones, president and CEO of Spirit Innovations, a uniform company based in Dallas.

Shoes are another important part of the uniform, not just for fashion but also for function and safety. Athletic shoe companies such as Nike and Reebok have developed shoes specifically for cheerleaders. These shoes support the foot and provide shock absorption for the demands of tumbling, jumping, and stunting. Companies like Nfinity Shoes design and manufacture shoes exclusively for cheerleaders, proving the need for a shoe made for what cheerleaders do. There are shoes for running, walking, tennis, and basketball that address the needs of those athletes, and shoe companies recognize that cheerleaders also require a shoe just for cheerleading.

Makeup

The crowd in a football stadium, gymnasium, or competition arena can be several hundred feet away from the cheerleaders, making it difficult to see details like the mouth and eyes. Performance makeup solves the problem. It brightens the face and defines facial features so that the crowd can see the smiles and expressions of the cheerleaders.

Makeup application in cheer-leading becomes theatrical. Glitter makeup and temporary tattoos of stars and team mascots are especially popular with competition teams and for special performances. Makeup can even match uniform colors and themes.

Makeup application varies by the place, time, and type of performance, and it is always dictated by the amount of light in the performance area. When cheering at sporting events, the makeup is applied heavier than it is in everyday circumstances. From a distance, and under stadium lights, face color washes out. Bright cheeks and lips and well-defined eyes will still look natural in these settings.

At competitions, the look can be more dramatic to match team uniforms that are more decorated and flashy. Specially formulated glitter makeup, colors that coordinate with uniform colors, and stencils in the shapes of stars and mascots make a competition face exciting.

CHAPTER 5

Cheerleading and You

Especially as a new cheerleader, training puts new challenges on your body that it either hasn't experienced before or isn't used to. Learning new tumbling, stunting, and dancing techniques will cause muscle groups to be used in new ways. While soreness is normal, a cheerleader has to be careful to listen to his or her body for signs of injury or weakness so that modifications can be made to the training regimen.

Perfecting cheerleading skills is only part of what it takes to be a great cheerleader. Cross-training, maintaining a healthy diet, and being careful to avoid injuries are also important.

Staying Healthy

Training to be a cheerleader and training as a cheerleader require that the athlete take extra care of his or her body. Staying healthy is a balance of conditioning, eating a well-balanced diet, drinking plenty of water, and getting enough sleep. A lot of energy is expended during practice and has to be replaced.

A well-balanced diet for a cheerleader includes lean meats, fruits, dairy, vegetables, and whole grains. It emphasizes protein to feed muscles and provide long-term energy. At least eight eight-ounce glasses of water are recommended daily; twice as much is needed when training is especially intense. Eight hours of sleep each night will allow muscles to rest and repair for more work the next day!

Avoiding Injuries

The first rule of avoiding injuries is properly warming up before every practice and performance. Light aerobic exercise to raise the heart rate followed by stretching the major muscle groups that will be worked will warm the muscles and prepare the body for work.

The second rule of avoiding injuries is skill progression and execution with correct technique. Every cheerleader wants to perform difficult tumbling and stunts, and a thorough knowledge and mastering of the basics must come first. The most simple arm motion, forward roll, and stunting technique actually prepare the body for more advanced skills. Proper training, repetition, and patience are the only way to get there.

The third rule of avoiding injuries is safety. A cheerleading coach must be properly trained to teach, spot, and correct skills. Every cheerleader must remain aware of not only what he or she is doing but also what teammates are doing. This will help them avoid falls and drops.

Cross Training

Training in supplemental sports and techniques will create a well-rounded and strong cheerleader. A combination of aerobic exercise, anaerobic exercise, strength training, and stretching provides the total body conditioning necessary for cheer routines.

Aerobic exercise builds stamina for cheering through an entire football game or basketball game. Cheerleaders have to be able to maintain motion technique, enunciate the words of the cheers so the

Weight training is just one part of overall conditioning for cheerleaders; it helps build the strength needed for stunting and tumbling. A well-rounded weight regimen that works the major muscle groups of both the upper and lower body is ideal for cheerleaders.

crowd can understand what they're saying, and keep their energy up for several hours. Aerobic conditioning prepares cheerleaders for this kind of activity level. Examples of aerobic exercise include running, swimming, cycling, rope jumping, and various types of exercise classes.

The purpose of anaerobic exercise is to condition the body to maintain a high level of energy for a short period of time. A competition routine is a good example of the need for short bursts of high energy. Cheerleaders need to make it through a two-minute and thirty-second routine with peak energy and without becoming overly winded. Anaerobic training includes running wind sprints, running stairs, sprinting on a bicycle, and speed skating.

Strength training is important to cheerleaders particularly for stunting and tumbling. Bases and spotters need solid leg and arm strength to lift and support flyers. Tumbling requires powerful legs and arms, and strong core muscles to throw and control various skills. Strength training through the use of free weights, weight machines, and resistance bands and tubing all target and develop the specific muscle groups required for cheerleading skills.

Stretching lengthens the muscles, keeps the body flexible, and, as part of the warm-up, prepares the body for more difficult work. Stretching also helps prevent injury. Tumbling, dance, and stunting all require flexibility. Daily stretching, incorporated both into a warm-up and a cooldown for at least fifteen to thirty minutes at a time, will keep the muscles pliable and healthy.

Keeping in Shape

Just like a student has to study to maintain good grades, a cheerleader has to practice healthy eating and exercise habits daily to stay in shape. During the cheerleading season, a good coach will put his or her team on a regimen that includes a healthy eating plan, aerobic and anaerobic training, strength training, and stretching to develop the most well-rounded, conditioned athletes. Off-season, it takes personal motivation and discipline to maintain a conditioning schedule on your own. You can team up with conditioning partners to encourage and keep track of each other's progress. You can join a gym and take classes in yoga and Pilates to support the strength and aerobic training you do on your own. Staying in shape is a lifelong commitment. It's actually a lifestyle, and it's totally up to you to choose and stay committed to it.

Benefits for Your Future

In addition to the healthful benefits that cheerleading brings, participation in the sport offers a wealth of opportunities, such as scholarships. Cheerleaders may also transfer the skills and discipline they develop to careers in sports, whether or not they are connected to the spirit arts. Companies like to hire people who are dedicated team players, able to maintain a positive attitude during times of stress. These are all qualities that are reinforced on cheerleading squads. Many successful people, including actors, pop stars, members of Congress, presidents, and even a Supreme Court justice, are former cheerleaders.

College Scholarships

Recognizing that cheerleading is an athletic activity or sport, many colleges and universities are awarding scholarships to their cheerleaders. Scholarships range from book allowances to tuition to room and board. According to *American Cheerleader's Scholarship Guide*, more than 230 colleges and universities offer incentives to cheerleaders. A complete state-by-state listing can be found online at

Famous Former Cheerleaders

From actors and actresses to singers, news anchors, comedians, and even U.S. presidents, an impressive list of famous people were once cheerleaders!

Paula Abdul	Kathy Griffin
Kirstie Alley	Teri Hatcher
Courtney Cox Arquette	Faith Hill
Toni Basil	Lauryn Hill
Angela Bassett	Samuel L. Jackson
Halle Berry	Ashley Judd
Sandra Bullock	Jessica Lange
George W. Bush	Madonna
Jamie Lee Curtis	Cheri Oteri
Cameron Diaz	Franklin Roosevelt
Michael Douglas	Alicia Silverstone
Calista Flockhart	Meryl Streep
Ruth Bader Ginsburg	Renee Zellweger

http://www.americancheerleader.com or in the *Coach's Handbook*, published annually by *American Cheerleader*.

Careers

While it's not realistic to think that you will cheer forever, it is very realistic to create a way to turn your passion into a career. From the

Being a cheerleader teaches life skills that prepare you for college and beyond. From building friendships and learning to work as part of a team to leadership skills and self-confidence, cheerleading gives girls and boys skill sets necessary to succeed in nearly any endeavor in life.

obvious options of coaching and teaching to the more obscure choices like Web site designer, graphic artist, fashion designer, writer, and even photographer, your cheer career doesn't have to end when you hang up your pom pons.

GLOSSARY

aerobics Exercise that increases stamina.

all-star gym A training facility for competitive cheerleaders.

anaerobic Relating to exercise that increases the ability to perform at high energy for short bursts of time.

chant A short, repetitive phrase cheerleaders use to encourage and lead crowd involvement.

cheer A series of phrases, motions, and stunts that a cheerleading squad performs.

choreography Dance steps, cheer motions, and other techniques put together to form a routine.

jumps A variety of jumping techniques unique to cheerleaders.

megaphone A device used for projecting voices so the crowd can hear and respond to chants led by a cheer squad.

motions A series of arm positions used in cheers and chants.

pom pon Invented by Lawrence Herkimer, colorful bunches of plastic streamers used by cheerleaders and dance teams to accentuate choreography.

spirit sign A sign used by cheerleaders during a chant or cheer to lead a crowd through a response. It can be used to spell school initials or words like "go," "fight," or "win."

spring floor A gymnastics mat laid over a floor made of wood or composite, and mounted on a series of springs. It is designed to provide additional shock absorption and safety for tumbling and stunting.

squad A group of cheerleaders organized to raise school spirit or for competitive purposes.

stunt A skill where three or more cheerleaders mount or climb to build a group or pyramid. Stunts can involve tumbling and tossing.

tumbling Gymnastics skills used as part of a cheer routine or performance.

yell leaders The first term used to describe a group that encouraged spectators at athletic events to "yell along" in support of the team.

For More Information

American Association of Cheerleading Coaches and Advisors (AACCA)
6745 Lenox Center Court, Suite 318
Memphis, TN 38115
(800) 533-6583
Web site: http://www.aacca.org

National All-Star Cheerleading Coaches Congress (NACCC)
6745 Lenox Center Court, Suite 300

Memphis, TN 38115

Web site: http://www.nacccongress.com

National Council for Spirit Safety and Education (NCSSE)

P.O. Box 311192

Enterprise, AL 36331–1192

(866) 456-2773

Web site: http://www.spiritsafety.com

United States All-Star Federation (USASF)

6745 Lenox Center Court, Suite 300

Memphis, TN 38115

(800) 829-6237

e-mail: lstella@usasf.net

Web site: http://www.usasf.net

Web Sites

Due to the changing nature of Internet links, the Rosen Publishing Group, Inc., has developed an online list of Web sites related to the subject of this book. This site is updated regularly. Please use this link to access the list:

http://www.rosenlinks.com/team/cheer

For Further Reading

Coachman, Mary Kaye. *Dance Team* (Team Spirit!). New York, NY: Rosen Publishing Group, 2007.

Golden, Suzi J. *101 Best Cheers: How to Be the Best Cheerleader Ever*. Mahwah, NJ: Troll Communications, 2001.

Headridge, Pam, and Nancy Garr. *Developing a Successful Cheerleading Program*. Monterey, CA: Coaches Choice Books, 2004.

Peters, Craig. *Techniques of Cheerleading* (Let's Go Team Series: Cheer, Dance, March). Broomall, PA: Mason Crest Publishers, 2003.

Spirit Direct. *The Team Book*. Dallas, TX: Spirit Direct, 2000.

Tecco, Betsy Dru. *Food for Fuel: The Connection Between Food and Physical Activity*. New York, NY: Rosen Publishing Group, 2007.

Wilson, Leslie. *The Ultimate Guide to Cheerleading: For Cheerleaders and Coaches*. New York, NY: Three Rivers Press, 2003.

Bibliography

About.com. "Famous Cheerleaders." Retrieved August 24, 2005 (http://cheerleading.about.com/od/famouscheerleaders).

Corbin, Jill Marie, and Lynn Singer. "100 Years of Cheer: A Celebration of Spirit." *American Cheerleader*, February 1998, pp. 33–37.

Drillsandskills.com. "Floor." Retrieved August 30, 2005 (http://www.drillsandskills.com/skills/Floor).

Jones, Kevin. *America's Best Summer Camp Book*. Dallas, TX: America's Best Cheer & Dance, 2001.

National All-Star Cheerleading Coaches Congress. "2005–06 Glossary." Retrieved August 23, 2005 (http://www.nacccongress.com/pdf/Glossary0-06.pdf).

Spirit Direct. *The Team Book*. Dallas, TX: Spirit Direct, 2000.

Index

About the Author

Lynn Singer is the vice president of sales and marketing for America's Best Cheer & Dance, Inc., and Spirit Innovations. She is also the creator of Camp-In-A-Box™, a multimedia training resource for dance teams and cheerleaders. Singer sits on the editorial advisory board for *Inside Cheerleading* magazine. Her twenty-two years of experience in the spirit industry include having served as editor of *In Motion* magazine as well as senior contributing editor of *Dance Spirit, American Cheerleader, Dance Teacher Now,* and *Stage Directions* magazines. She was inducted into the United Performing Association's Hall of Fame, served as vice president of NCA Danz, and has traveled nationally and internationally as a teacher, guest speaker, coordinator, and adjudicator of dance and cheerleading events. Singer lives in Dallas, Texas, with her husband David, two border collies named Fly and Sweep, and a cat named Tigger.

Series Consultant: Susan Epstein

Photo Credits

Cover, pp. 1, 32, 46 Fairport High School; p. 5 © Kelly Mooney/Corbis; p. 7 © Tony Arruza/Corbis; p. 8 © Louie Psihoyos/Corbis; pp. 9, 16, 18, 33, 40, 48 Cheerleaders of America; p. 11 © Underwood & Underwood/Corbis; p. 13 National Cheerleaders Association; pp. 15, 56 Frederick Douglass High School; p. 21 © Dennis MacDonald/Photo Edit; p. 24 © Greg Flume/Corbis; p. 27 Icon SMI/Corbis; p. 28 © Dean Conger/Corbis; pp. 35, 49 Eastern Cheerleaders Association; p. 37 © Marc Asnin/Corbis Saba; pp. 41, 43 America's Best Championships; p. 50 © Saed Hindash/Star Ledger/Corbis; p. 52 © Simon Plant/zefa/Corbis.

Designer: Gene Mollica; Editor: Wayne Anderson; Photo Researcher: Marty Levick